THE
BATTLE OF BRITAIN
MEMORIAL FLIGHT

THE
BATTLE OF BRITAIN
MEMORIAL FLIGHT

Richard Winslade

Osprey Colour Series

Published in 1987 by Osprey Publishing Limited
27A Floral Street, London WC2E 9DP
Member company of the George Philip Group

British Library Cataloguing in Publication Data

Winslade, Richard
    Battle of Britain Memorial Flight.—
    (Osprey colour series)
    1. Great Britain. *Royal Air Force. Battle of Britain
    Memorial Flight*
    —Pictorial works
    I. Title
    358.4'3   UG635.G7

ISBN 0-85045-724-6

Editor Dennis Baldry
Designed by David Tarbutt
Printed in Hong Kong

Front cover BBMF formation consisting of Lancaster, Hurricane (to starboard) and Spitfire.

Title pages Spitfire IIa P7350 silhouetted during engine ground-running tests in the winter of 1985

Preceding pages The author ensconced in the rear turret of PA474, as seen by the camera of Flt Lt Bob Burden from a Tornado F.2

Richard Winslade runs an advertising photography studio and specializes in large format still-life subjects. He took up aviation photography in 1972 under the expert guidance of the late Neil Williams, who guided him through the pitfalls of his first commission in this field, which was to illustrate an article on aerobatics. Since then Richard Winslade's work has appeared in most of the leading aviation magazines. He works closely with both the BBMF and the Royal Navy Historic Flight and illustrates their annual brochures.

This book would not have been possible without the generous help of the BBMF and the author is deeply grateful to everyone who assisted.

Contents

'The Bomber' 8

Black and blue 42

Hurricane: the forgotten fighter? 56

Spitfire: the power and the glory 68

TLC 94

Flypast 114

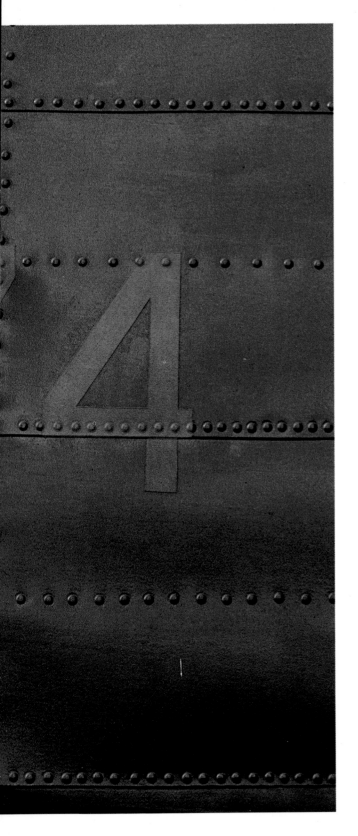

'The Bomber'

Avro Lancaster B Mk 1 PA474 was built by
Vickers Armstrongs at Chester in 1945 equipped
for Tiger Force operations in the Far East, but
Japan surrendered before any B.1 (FE) aircraft
were despatched. After a spell as a photographic
survey aircraft in Africa, she was flown back to
England and used for laminar-flow wing research
at Cranfield. PA474 was subsequently stored at
Wroughton and earmarked for the RAF Museum
at Hendon in north London. Shortage of space
prompted a move to Henlow in 1964, and it was
here that members of No 44 Sqn—a Vulcan
bomber unit on the look-out for a gate guardian—
realized that the Lanc could be made airworthy.
Permission for 'one flight only' back to their home
base at Waddington was only the beginning and
she joined the BBMF in 1973. **Above** Slowly,
carefully, 'The Bomber' begins to emerge

These pages and overleaf The Lancaster is a tight fit inside the BBMF's hangar—a wing span of 102 ft (31.1 m) leaves little room for manoeuvre. Other vital statistics include a length of 69 ft 4 in (21.1 m); a height of 19 ft 7 in (5.97 m); and a maximum takeoff weight (standard display) of 47,000 lb (21,367 kg) with seven crew and a typical fuel uplift of around 650–850 Imp gal (2954–3863 lit). For comparison, the wartime overload with a 22,000 lb Grand Slam supersonic 'earthquake' bomb was 70,000 lb (31,750 kg)

Left All too often Murphy's Law dictates that as soon as the aircraft is towed out into the open, the weather takes a turn for the worse. With the sky darkening behind, PA474 waits for her crew to arrive. The Frazer Nash Mk 5 nose turret was located at No 1451 (Haverhill) Sqn, Air Training Corps, and exchanged for a dummy Fireflash air-to-air missile. **Above** JT Mike Hall keeps a watchful eye on proceedings as the aircraft is towed out. **Below** The Lancaster has a long and close association with the 'Bomber County' of Lincolnshire—hence the Coat of Arms of the City of Lincoln. Much to the disappointment of some ex-Bomber Command veterans, the bomb symbols which once adorned the forward fuselage were removed

In common with other B Mk 1s, PA474 was fitted with Rolls-Royce or Packard Merlin 20s or 22s, each rated at 1460 hp. Today, however, the aircraft is powered by a wide variety of Merlin marks: No 1 (port outer) is a Merlin 502 from a York, the transport relative of the Lanc; No 2 (port inner) is a Merlin 500-29 from a CASA 2111, the Spanish-built version of the Heinkel He 111 bomber; No 3 (starboard inner) is a Canadian Packard 225 from a Mosquito; while No 4 (starboard outer) also came off a York. No 3 is always started first—it drives the air compressor which breathes life into the wheel brakes and radiator shutters. The bomb doors are closed to check the hydraulic pump after No 3 is running smoothly at 1200 rpm. To allow safe access to each engine in the event of a fire the start-up sequence is 3, 4, 2 and 1. **Left** Flame-damper shrouds are no longer fitted over the exhaust ejectors. The O-shaped mesh grille is the anti-ice guard for the carburettor intake

This page and overleaf Chocks away: the bomb doors are closed and the engines are running sweetly. Oil/radiator temperatures are stabilized at 60°C and 80°C respectively, though the Packard tends to run a little hotter

Left A pair of Tornado GR.1s overshoot as the Lanc holds before receiving takeoff clearance. After checking the magnetos at static boost and slow running checks, the throttles are reset to 1200 rpm. Takeoff vital actions are elevator trim $3\frac{1}{2}$ divisions nose-down, fuel tanks selected, booster pumps for Nos 1 and 2 tanks on, crossfeed cock off, and radiator shutters set to automatic. Finally, the air intakes are checked in cold air and the superchargers in low gear. The Lancaster tends to swing to port on takeoff, so the left-hand power levers are advanced slightly ahead until the rudders gain sufficient authority. Unstick is normally achieved at 112 mph (180 km/h)

Above Viewed from the astrodome just aft of the cockpit, RAF Coningsby recedes into the distance as the aircraft flies a smart left-hand circuit at about 250 ft (75 m) leaving an unmistakeable shadow on the field below

The Frazer Nash Mk 150 mid-upper turret was discovered at a gunnery school in Argentina (it had never been fitted to an aircraft) and came back to Britain aboard the County class destroyer HMS *Hampshire* in 1973

Left A gunner's eye view of Normandy from the mid-upper turret. The chinagraph pencil numbers on the Perspex were added during the aircraft's winter overhaul at Abingdon to facilitate accurate re-assembly

The commanding officer of the Flight is by tradition the captain of 'The Bomber'. Sqn Ldr Scott Anderson (left) keeps a sharp lookout off the island of Jersey before being called in for the BBMF slot in the display programme. This picture was taken in May 1984 and command of the Flight has since passed into the capable hands of Sqn Ldr Tony Banfield

This page and overleaf PA474 differs from wartime Lancasters in that it has a seat for a copilot. This not only eases the workload on the captain but also makes training new pilots much easier. Sqn Ldr Bill Houldsworth (above) checks the time to run-in for a display in the Channel Islands. Relevant information such as radio frequencies and slot times are written on his kneeboard, which is just visible at the bottom of the picture. Bill Houldsworth served on Lancasters, Halifaxes Neptunes, Hastings and Shackletons before joining the BBMF. He was awarded the MBE in 1983 and collected the CBE when he retired at the end of 1984

Lost in Holland! The Lancaster is flown VFR (Visual Flight Rules) with the aid of a 1:250,000 map, a stopwatch, and mental arithmetic. The pilot also receives position updates over the RT. Flt Lt Dick Cave is 'lost in Holland' during the Operation Manna Forty trip the Flight made in 1985 to commemorate the dropping of food supplies to starving civilians at the end of WW2

Right Lost in France! Flt Lt Doug Eke served with the Flight for two years as its adjutant and navigator, roles which also include fine-tuning the arrangements for displays with airshow organizers and finding accommodation for the Flight if they land away from base. With a map of northern France in hand, Doug Eke navigates the aircraft from Jersey to Cherbourg for a flypast during the D-Day anniversary celebrations on 6 June 1984

RAF kid flying gloves are world famous and it is unwise to leave them unattended. The instrument on the left is a turn/slip indicator

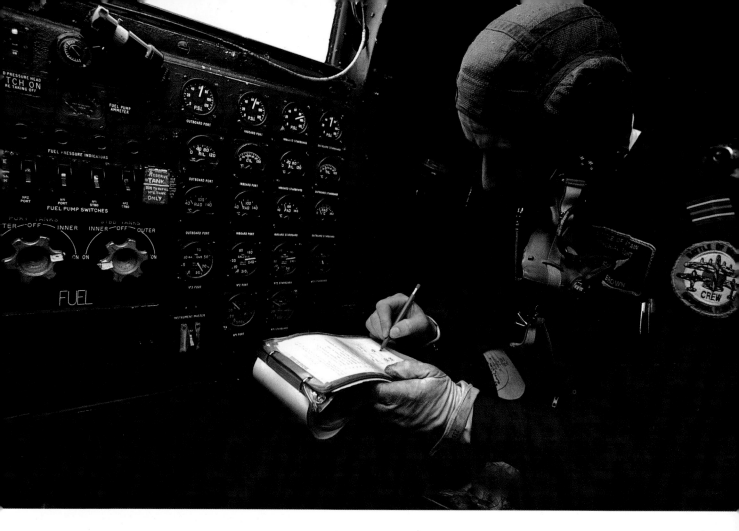

Flt Lt Nigel Brown is one of the three flight
engineers who take it in turns to fly in the
aircraft. His control panel is just behind the
copilot and he monitors the smooth running (or
otherwise) of the engines from a rather
uncomfortable bench-type seat

Above JT Mike Hall sits next to the radio compartment during his first trip in the Lancaster. **Opposite page** The original radio equipment is no longer used for its intended purpose, but it adds a welcome air of authenticity. About 80 per cent of the interior is pure WW2-Lancaster. Communication is maintained by modern VHF/UHF radios operated by the navigator

Right Sgt Rick Evans fast asleep on the main spar during a transit flight. One of the Flight's airframe technicians, he and his colleagues have been known to work through the night to meet the deadline for a flying display. The main spar of the Lancaster is a notorious obstacle which often infuriated the wartime crews who had to clamber over it in their bulky flying kit, especially when they had to abandon the aircraft in pitch darkness

Facing forward in the mid-upper turret gives one
the impression of riding on top of an airborne
express train. **Right** Cpl Peter Jeffery ('Gerbs')
practices shooting down our fighter escort (Spitfire
IIa P7350) off the coast of Guernsey

Two contrasting views from the mid-upper turret:
Above Looking out at the starboard wing and
Right facing aft with the coast of Normandy in
the background. The muzzle of one of the twin
.303 Browning machine guns can be seen at top
left

Far right Awesome Avro: PA474 heads for RAF
Finningley near Doncaster in the summer of 1986
to attend one of the UK's biggest air shows—Sqn
Ldr Tony Banfield is at the controls. To ease the
maintenance burden the hydraulic power system
for the gun turrets has been removed, and the
turrets have to be traversed manually

En route to Coningsby after her major overhaul at Abingdon in 1984, a refit which included repainting the aircraft to be externally representative of a Bomber Command Lancaster operated by No 101 Sqn, coded SR-D

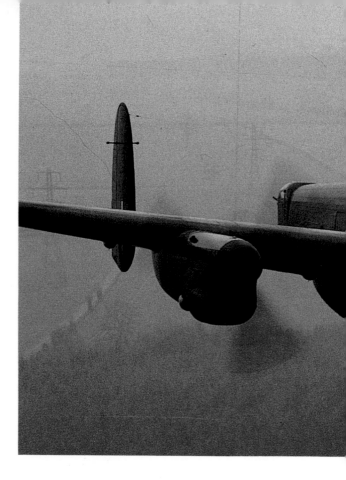

Taxying at Jersey in September 1984 with the port inner sick due to ignition problems. After a more serious recurrence at St Athan the Flight's trusty Chipmunk arrived with a new wiring harness

Overleaf When this photograph was taken on her way home from Manston in 1982, PA474 was representative of AJ-G, Wg Cdr Guy Gibson's aircraft in which he led No 617 Sqn on the famous Dams Raid in 1943. The Lancaster first flew in Manchester III guise in early 1941, serialled BT308, and total production (including 430 in Canada by Victory Aircraft) reached 7377, of which 3349 were lost on wartime operations. When these words were written (October 1986) PA474 was the world's only Lancaster maintained in flying condition, but the Canadian Warplane Heritage hope to have their Mk X FM213 back in the air sometime in 1987

Black and blue

The Battle of Britain Memorial Flight was formed at the famous Fighter Command airfield at Biggin Hill, Kent, in 1957 to commemorate the major battle honour of the Royal Air Force and to act as a reminder of the critical importance of the Service to Britain's defences. Since then the Flight has acquired nine aircraft, consisting of four Spitfires (a IIa, a Vb, and two PR Mk XIX), two Hurricane IIcs, a Lancaster B.1, a Devon C.2, and a Chipmunk T.10. The BBMF fly about 145 displays per year compared, say, to the Red Arrows' average of 85. **Left** BBMF crew patch

Top right You don't have to be mad to work here, but it helps! A manic Flt Lt Jim Wild mucks in to help with menial tasks like helping to close the hangar doors after the days flying is done. He joined the RAF as an instrument fitter in 1958, trained as a pilot in 1966, and went on to fly Lightnings and Tornados

Right Sqn Ldr Paul Day is probably the most experienced current Spitfire pilot in the world today, with over 300 hours on type. He is the fighter training officer of the Flight, and an air-combat instructor on Phantoms with No 228 OCU at Coningsby with over 3000 hours on the mighty F-4. His American flying jacket is something of a trademark—slick shades complete the macho effect. A bewildered Jim Wild looks on

Sqn Ldr Paul Day straps in to Spitfire PR Mk
XIX PM631, assisted by the ever-watchful
electrical technician Cpl Paul Wheal who, in
common with the other groundcrew, doubles and
triples in a variety of roles to get the aircraft
airborne for a display

Flt Lt Jack Hamill settles down in the back seat of the Chipmunk before a continuation training flight. 2000 of Hamill's 5000 flying hours are on Phantoms. It's important for the pilot's to remain familiar with the handling quirks of piston-engined 'tail-draggers' after flying fast-jets, and the 'Chippy' is a cost-effective substitute for the Flight's precious metal

Far left Flown by Flt Lt Mark Robinson, Chipmunk T.10 WK518 chugs down the display line at Duxford, the Cambridgeshire home of the Imperial War Museum's huge collection of historic aircraft. Apart from being a delightful continuation trainer, the Chippy also flies occasional reconnaissance missions to check the suitability of new display sites

Left The Devon entered RAF service in 1948 for staff transport and communications duties. Powered by a pair of 380-hp Gipsy Queens, the aircraft has a top speed of 230 mph (370 km/h) and a range of 880 miles (1415 km). The Flight's example, VP981, has flown some 9000 hours

Below Devon preflight: Sqn Ldr Scott Anderson, MBE, was Officer Commanding BBMF for three years until he retired from the RAF after the 1985 display season. He is currently flying Trislanders with Aurigny Airlines in Jersey. The de Havilland Devon C.2 is a recent recruit which has eased the burden of supporting the Flight on distant detachments, when the groundcrew and spares can't all fit into the Lancaster

SAC Vince Carter adds a touch of Sparkle to the Lancaster. **Inset** A basic tool kit is carried on every sortie

Hey, wait for me! After helping to make sure that all was well during the start-up sequence, Cpl Ian Hinks sprints aboard the Lancaster as it prepares to taxi out behind the Chippy for the return trip from Duxford to Coningsby. Your intrepid correspondent wasn't far behind.

JT Mike Hall removes the protective cover from one of the main wheels of the Lancaster. Leaking oil and hydraulic fluid can easily rot the tyres

Flt Lt Mark Robinson takes a turn at refuelling
the Lancaster. Fuel uplifts of over 1000 Imp gal
(4545 lit) are not uncommon, giving the Lanc an
endurance in excess of five hours; she burns about
200 Imp gal (909 lit) per hour during a display

During the course of the air display season members of the Flight are required to meet and entertain people from many walks of life, and equal care and interest is shown to all. Sqn Ldr Paul Day (right of picture) and Flt Lt Jack Hamill escort King Hussein of Jordan and Air Chief Marshal Sir Alisdair Steedman at the 1985 International Air Tattoo (IAT) at Fairford in Gloucestershire

Well done! Flt Lt Jim Wild is congratulated by
the Boss (Scott Anderson) after his first flight in
the Hurricane in the spring of 1985. Jim Wild
modestly admits that he never thought his
schoolboy dream of flying the Hurricane would
actually come true. Pilots become eligible to fly
the 'baby Spits' (the Mk IIa and Vb) after
building 15 hours (including display flying) on the
Hurricane. Similarly, after 15 hours on the
Spitfire IIa/Vb, pilots are given the chance to fly
the Griffon-engined PR Mk XIXs

Left Cpl Peter 'Gerbs' Jeffery is one of the most knowledgeable airframe technicians, quoting parts lists and reference numbers from memory as required. He is at his oil-stained best troubleshooting problems

Below Cpl Downer joined the Flight in 1982. His skills as a communications technician were obviously not needed at Woodford in June 1985, where he had time to share a joke with Paul Day

Right A future RAF pilot gets the low down on the BBMF from Flt Lt Tim Nolan. Children are ardent admirers of the Flight's aeroplanes, which they seem to find more fascinating than the 'heavy metal' combat aircraft of today. At air shows, stickers and brochures are handed out in a constant stream

Hurricane: the forgotten fighter?

Left The prototype Hawker Hurricane made its maiden flight on 6 November 1935, the first of 14,533 (including 1451 Canadian Mk Xs) manufactured before production ceased in 1944. PZ865, one of two Mk IIcs in the BBMF and the last Hurricane to be built, is on her return flight from Brooklands (near Weybridge in Surrey) in November 1985, after attending the celebrations held to mark the type's fiftieth anniversary

Above The BBMF's other IIc is LF363, possibly the last example to enter RAF service (January 1944). She served with Nos 63, 309, and 26 Sqns and on various station flights until rescued by Hawker Aircraft and rebuilt. LF363 returned to Biggin Hill in 1956 and became one of the Flight's original aircraft. The 12-volt trolley-acc is being connected prior to start-up

Left Cpl Ian Hinks 'pulling through' to make sure that no excess oil is blocking the cylinder heads (which would otherwise blow off when the engine fired), and build up compression to help the electric starter. Propellers should always be treated as live—this task demands care and experience

Right Visible in the rear-view mirror, Flt Lt Jack Hamill receives the benefit of Sqn Ldr Paul Day's invaluable advice before his first flight in the Hurricane. **Above** What a beautiful noise! All Jack Hamill has to do now is bring her back in one piece

Overleaf Sapphire-blue flames spurt from the exhaust ejectors as LF363's Merlin 502 (ex-York) is given a nighttime run-up. Painted matt-black overall, the aircraft wears the VY-X codes of No 85 Sqn, a Hurricane night-fighter unit

The BBMF is by means the first RAF unit to operate the Hurricane IIc minus armour plate and armament, one wartime example being 1695 BDF (N) at Dalton in Scotland, a unit tasked with nocturnal fighter affiliation exercises against the air-gunners of Bomber Command. Flt Lt Peter Bouch 'attacks' the Lancaster as Spitfire IIa P7350 breaks away underneath

The two Hurricanes are normally flown at around 172–207 mph (277–333 km/h), compared to a wartime maximum of 335 mph (540 km/h) armed with four 20 mm Hispano cannon

Overleaf Wg Cdr John Ward at the controls of Hurricane IIc PZ865 *The Last of the Many!* The aircraft burns approximately 40 Imp gal (181 lit) per hour cruising at 172 mph (277 km/h)

The Last of the Many! enjoyed a long and happy career with Hawker Aircraft, being used for various trials, communications duties, air racing (her best result was a second place in the 1950 Kings Cup), and air displays. After being completely refurbished, PZ865 was presented to the Flight by Hawker Siddeley Aviation in 1974. Interestingly, the aircraft is fitted with long-range fuel tanks in the space previously used for 20 mm ammunition stowage. Her Merlin 25 came off a Mosquito. Despite the outstanding performance of the Hurricane during the Battle of Britain in 1940, when it equipped 32 Fighter Command squadrons, compared with $18\frac{1}{2}$ Spitfire squadrons, and scored more victories than all the other defences combined, the aircraft seems forever destined to fly under the shadow of the Spitfire's elliptical wings

Spitfire: the power and the glory

Left A classic study of Spitfire Mk IIa P7350, an aircraft which still bears the scars of battle—four patches cover bullet holes in her wings. Built at Castle Bromwich in 1940, P7350 served with Nos 616, 64, 266, and 603 Sqns

Above Identified by his low-visibility 'bone dome', Sqn Ldr Paul Day starts Spitfire Mk Vb AB910. Like P7350, this aircraft is powered by a 1280 hp Merlin 35 from a Boulton Paul Balliol T.2, the ill-conceived advanced trainer which entered RAF service in 1951

Left Flt Lt Merv Paine flies Spitfire Mk Vb
AB910 over typical Suffolk countryside in
somewhat overcast weather, but the visibility soon
improves (above). If rain is forecast the Flight's
fighters stay in the hangar to prevent damage to
the paint and propellers

Overleaf The Merlin 35 installation in P7350;
Rolls-Royce delivered 150,000 Merlin engines by
the end of WW2 and versions were fitted to over
100 other types of aircraft

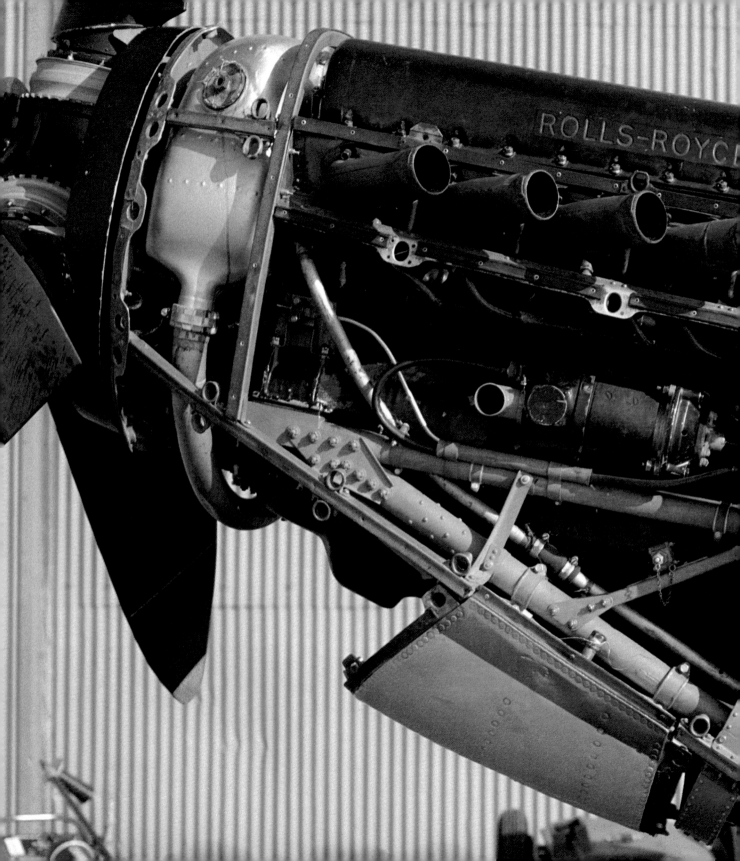

ELECTRICAL &
RADIO SOCKET

Tail safely secured (below) P7350 is tested by ground-running her 'new' Merlin 35, fitted during the winter months. The fuel tank in front of the cockpit holds 48 Imp gal (218 lit). **Above** Detail of the electrical and radio socket

Overleaf Piloted by Wg Cdr John Ward, P7350 is just north of Portsmouth on 5 March 1986 after attending the celebrations to mark the Spitfire's fiftieth birthday at Eastleigh airfield near Southampton, where 'Mutt' Summers made the maiden flight in K5054 back in 1936. Portchester Castle is in the background

Left The cockpit of P7350
Below P7350 straight and level over the English
Channel

Right Wg Cdr John Ward banks P7350 over the main runway at RNAS Lee-On-Solent

Overleaf En route to Coningsby in 1982, P7350 displays SH-D codes of No 64 Sqn

P7350 is painted to represent a Spitfire Mk IIa donated to No 41 Sqn by the Royal Observer Corps. During the war many RAF aircraft were paid for by public subscription, wealthy individuals, or various companies and organizations

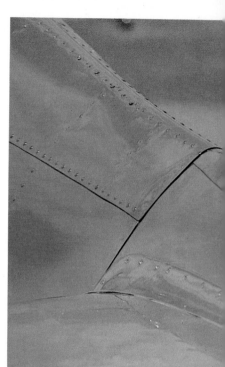

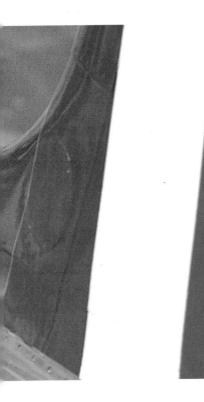

The differences in the construction of the Hurricane (top left) and the Spitfire are self-evident, but the Griffon-engined PR Mk XIX (top right and at left) also represents a huge advance of over the Merlin-engined Mk Vb (middle). Comparing a production Spitfire Mk 1 of 1938 and the post-war Seafire Mk 47 (a new aircraft entirely with different structure and shape, five-blade contra-rotating propellers, hydraulically folding wings, and four 20 mm cannon) we can see just how far the basic aircraft was developed by Joe Smith and his design team: the Mk 47 was 100 mph (161 km/h) faster, had 2.5 times the power, three times the range, double the rate of climb, double the firepower, and in terms of all-up weight it was equivalent to a Mk 1 carrying 32 passengers. In the space of ten years, 20,194 Spitfires and 2556 Seafires were manufactured; production peaked at 350 per month in 1944, mostly from the huge Castle Bromwich factory near Birmingham

A puff of white smoke and a lick of flame and Spitfire PR Mk XIX PM631 comes to life. Powered by a 2050-hp Griffon 61, the aircraft carries the codes DL-E of No 91 Sqn and prominent invasion stripes on the wings and fuselage

Left Sqn Ldr Paul Day tucked in immediately below the Lancaster's rear turret in PM631 and (above) turning over the Channel on the return leg of the Flight's annual outing to Jersey

The PR Mk XIX is possibly the most aesthetically pleasing of all the Griffon-engined variants. It is still instantly recognizable as a Spitfire—unlike, perhaps, the fundamentally redesigned post-war F.21 series. A PR Mk XIX flew the RAF's last operational Spitfire mission (Malaya, 1 April 1954) and, as part of the Woodvale Met Flight, the last RAF Spitfire sortie in 1957. PR Mk XIX production reached 225

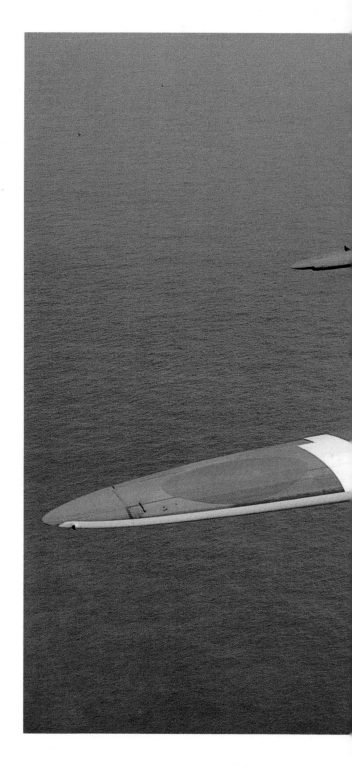

Overleaf, left Spitfire Mk IIa P7350, perhaps as seen by the enemy

Overleaf, right Ticket to ride. Flt Lt Dick Cave makes sure the tail stays firmly down during the long taxi to the crowd line at Woodford. The Lancaster is way out in front, approaching a Nimrod AEW.3. Not surprisingly, the big 2050-hp supercharged Griffon-engined marks are more tricky to fly than the earlier versions. Even more care is needed to contain swing on takeoff and the tendency to ground-loop on landing. On the ground, forward view is virtually non-existant and weaving is essential

TLC

Tender loving care and sheer hard work are the vital ingredients which keep the BBMF in the air. The maintenance staff of 13 strive with uncommon devotion, taking a justifiable pride in the immaculate condition in which the aircraft are invariably presented. **Left** The right tools can sometimes be as hard to find as aircraft spares. **Above** Engineering by committee: Cpl Jeffery has the situation under control, but an oil leak from a Hurricane attracts the usual crop of advice. **Overleaf** Spitfire PR Mk XIX PS915 in primer paint, under rebuild at Samlesbury by British Aerospace

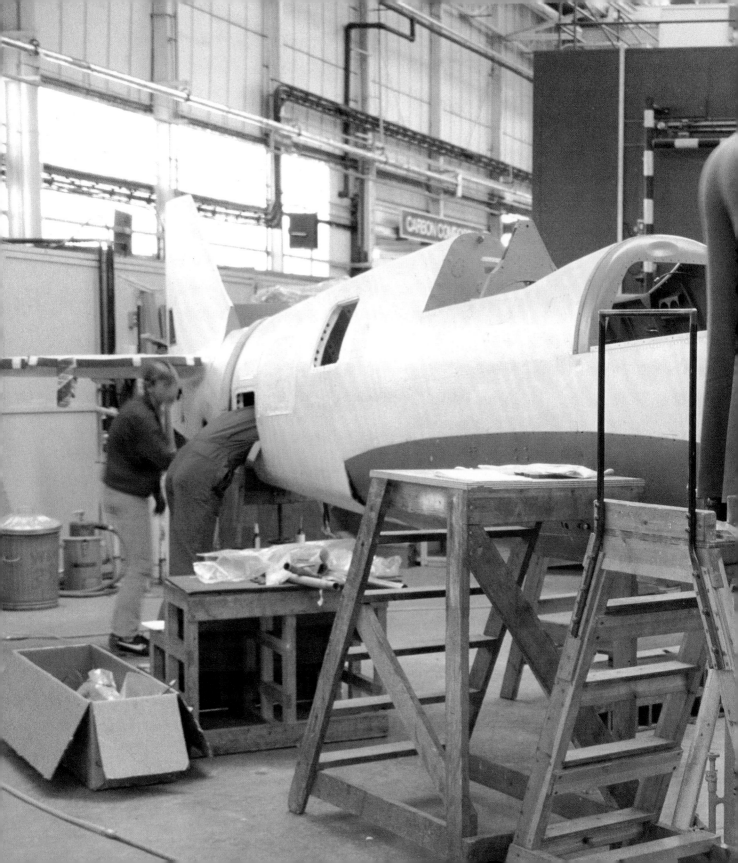

SAC Tim Hudson, a model of concentration

After the tail section and rear fuselage are mated, access is gained by squeezing through the entrance to the battery compartment. Also pictured overleaf, PS915 was delivered to the Central Photographic Reconnaissance unit at Benson, Oxfordshire, in 1945. Note the Canberra in the background, left of picture

Above Detail of the starboard wing, underside

Right PS915 is fitted with an ex-Shackleton Griffon 58 (Mod RG30SM5) specially adapted by Rolls-Royce to fit the propeller rating of the PR Mk XIX

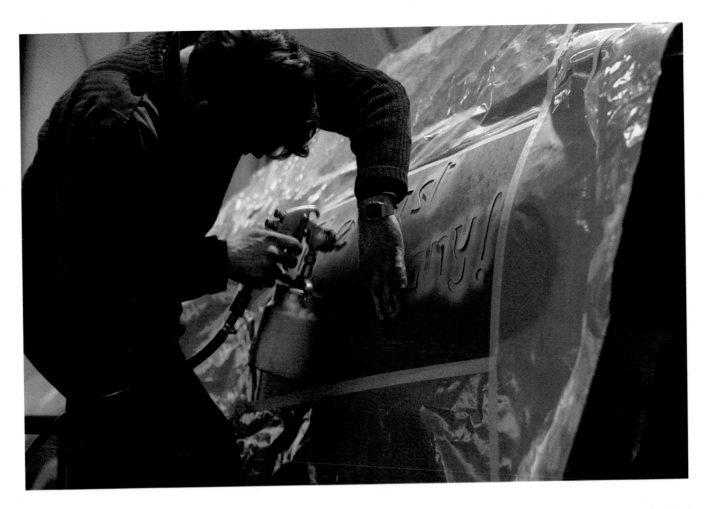

These pages and overleaf The aircraft are repainted every two years and the opportunity is usually taken to add new squadron codes. However, Hurricane PZ865 will always be *The Last of the Many!*—just as she emerged from the Hawker factory at Langley in August 1944. The Hurricanes are limited to 100 flying hours per year, but the Spits get 140

Left The Lancaster is equipped with a Frazer Nash Mk 121 tail-turret without its original Village Inn gun-laying radar. Cartridge-case ejection chutes are still fitted, and the rear navigation light remains near the base of the turret; wartime Lancasters also had a Monica tail-warning radar in this location. The turret's sliding clear vision panel is an ideal aid for air-to-air photography. **Right** The badge of the Air Gunners' Association.

Below To make the turret more hospitable (and the aircraft even more authentic), a wind deflector of wood and fabric construction was added in the winter of 1985 (see overleaf)

More work on the wind deflector. In a fast-jet air
force, it's not easy to find a craftsman familiar
with dope and fabric

After a thorough overhaul the mid-upper turret is lowered gently into position

Overleaf A general view of the Lancaster with her mid-upper turret now in place and the wind deflector complete prior to painting. PA474 is limited to 75 hours flying time per year; total time (at November 1986), approximately 3300 hours

Flypast

The Spitfire/Tornado display sequence was an instant success with airshow crowds when it was introduced during the 1985 season. Flown by Sqn Ldr Paul Day in the PR Mk XIX and Wg Cdr Richard Peacock-Edwards in the Tornado F.2, the double act was originally conceived by AVM Ken Hayr, AOC No 11 Group, RAF Strike Command. **Above** The one and only 'Spitnado' holds station behind the Lancaster en route for the IAT at Fairford

Overleaf Spitfire P7350 and Hurricane PZ865 (flown by Sqn Ldr Paul Day and Flt Lt Paul Rickard respectively) perform a more conventional duet

Left Spitfire salute: Wg Cdr John Ward leads Roland Fraissinet's beautiful PR Mk XI G-PRXI (PL983) and the late Honourable Patrick Lindsay's Mk Ia G-AIST (AR213), flown by Tony Bianchi. All three aircraft attended the Spitfire Society's eventful 50th anniversary celebrations at Eastleigh on 5 March 1986

Big friend, little friend 1: Lancaster and Spitfire in loose formation

Overleaf Big Friend, little friend 2: Lancaster and Hurricane over the flat landscape of Holland during the Operation Manna Forty trip

Preceding pages The Lancaster thunders over St Hellier in the Channel Islands

Standing in the wind-swept rear cockpit of the Swordfish operated by the Royal Navy Historic Flight, CPO Ron Gourlay, complete with Aldis Lamp, signals to the Lancaster before the flypast over the Arromanche Beach in Normandy for the D-Day celebrations on 6 June 1984. Because of the disparity in speed between the two aircraft, the Lancaster had to begin its run-in a good few miles behind the Swordfish to arrive over the display point at the same time

The Lancaster approaching the 'Stringbag' for the flypast. LS326 is currently the only airworthy Swordfish in the world, but Bob Spence is restoring Mk II/IV HS554 in Canada, and Strathallan is rejuvinating Mk II W5858

Overleaf The Flight arranged to overfly the Exocet-armed HMS *Scylla* off Guernsey after the Victory In Europe festivities in 1985. The frigate's engines have just gone astern, right on cue

Last page Coming soon, at an air display near you!